Ships

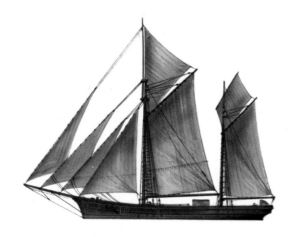

WARWICK PRESS

Contents

05629 GRISEWOOD AND DEMPSEY

Author   Jonathan Rutland
Editor   Michael Dempsey

Library of Congress Cataloging in Publication Data

Rutland, Jonathan.
    Ships.

    (Modern knowledge library)
    Includes index.

    SUMMARY: Discusses the history, design, and construction of
ships. Includes material on various ships developed such as steamships,
ferries, and hydrofoils.

    1. Ships—Juvenile literature.   [1. Ships]   I. Title.

VM150.R85   623.8   76–15007
ISBN 0–531–02447–4
ISBN 0–531–01199–2 lib. bdg.

First published in Great Britain by Sampson Low in 1975
Printed in Italy by New Interlitho, Milan

Ships

The earliest pictures found of boats are at least 6000 years old, but no doubt man made boats long before that – long before he could draw. Perhaps it all began with someone using a large piece of driftwood or a bunch of reeds to support himself in the water. Perhaps he, or his descendants, then discovered by chance that a hollow log was more buoyant than a solid one. Eventually he would have learned to tie bundles of sticks or reeds together to make a raft, and to improve on the hollow log by hollowing out a tree trunk himself. Later still he added an outrigger to stabilize his dugout – and a sail to both types of craft.

The raft was a built-up boat. From it may have developed the first real boats. The dugout proved in the long run a dead end. Beyond a certain size it becomes unworkable, but primitive peoples still use them, and have in the past made some astonishing voyages in them. Over 1000 years ago, the Polynesians crossed and re-crossed the Pacific Ocean in dugout canoes.

How a Ship Floats

For shipbuilders of today just as for early man, every ship must float easily and stay upright.

The first men to suggest building ships of metal were often laughed at. Yet Archimedes found out about buoyancy over 2000 years ago. He knew that if you fill a container to the brim with water, float a piece of wood in it, and measure the water that spills out (that is displaced), then you have found the displacement of the piece of wood. Archimedes found that an object which sinks displaces a volume of water equal to its own volume. One which floats displaces a volume of water equal to the volume of the object below the waterline. He worked out that a body in water is buoyed up by a force equal to the weight of the water it displaces.

A lump of metal is much more dense than water, and if placed in water it will sink. But if that same lump is hammered out into a bowl shape, it will float. The weight of the metal remains the same, but because the size of the new object (the bowl) is much greater, its density is much less. If you now fill the bowl slowly with water, the floating body becomes heavier and heavier. When its weight exceeds the weight of the water it displaces, it will sink as before.

Most ships have draft marks at bow and stern, from which the master can tell exactly how many tons of water his vessel is displacing – the weight of his ship plus everything aboard. This is known as the ship's displacement tonnage. Deadweight tonnage is

Above: Bulk ships are usually measured in deadweight tonnage, general cargo and passenger ships in gross tonnage, and warships in displacement tonnage. Top, the tanker ''Ardtaraig'', deadweight tonnage 214,128. Middle, the liner ''Canberra'', gross tonnage 44,807. Bottom, a naval ship, displacement tonnage 1900.

Below: The Ross Winans cigar ship launched in 1866. Its designers hoped that the vessel would slip through the water more easily and roll less than an ordinary ship. But its lack of stability made the cigar ship unsafe.

a measure of the number of tons (of cargo, crew, fuel etc.) which the ship can carry. Many general cargo and passenger ships are described by their gross tonnage, which is a measure of volume in units of 100 cubic feet. It stems from the time when a ship's capacity was measured by how many barrels (called *tuns*) of wine it could carry. Net tonnage is a measure of the volume of the ship's actual earning space, again in units of 100 cubic feet. It is the gross tonnage less the space taken up by, for example, the crew's quarters, the ship's machinery, and so on.

The other essential of every ship is stability. A ship must be so designed that when it heels over the force of gravity acting downward and the force of buoyancy acting upward combine to right the vessel. The diagrams on the right show a stable ship, an unstable ship and a cylindrical ship with zero stability.

In a stable ship gravity and buoyancy work together to right the heeling vessel. The force of buoyancy is greatest on that side of the ship which is most submerged.

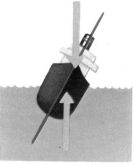

In an unstable ship gravity and buoyancy combine to capsize the heeling vessel. They both push it in the same direction.

In a cigar ship the forces of gravity and buoyancy act through the same point and cancel each other. There is no stability.

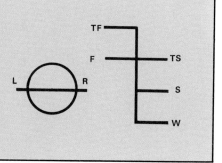

Load lines show the depth to which a ship sinks in the water when it is properly loaded. The circular mark is known (after its originator) as the Plimsoll Line. The left-hand marks on the other load line show the permitted levels in fresh water. The marks to the right are for salt water – TS tropical summer – S summer – W winter.

Designing a Ship

Safety and comfort at sea are governed by mathematics.

The photograph shows a ship with a ram bow. Designers have found that this shape reduces the drag of the hull, and as it gives a little extra buoyancy the ship can carry more cargo.

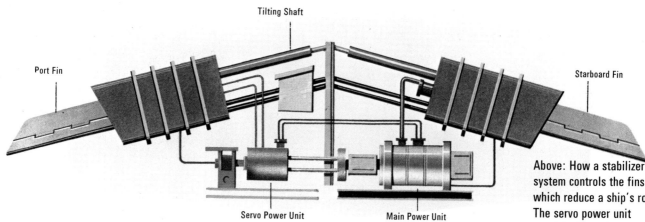

Port Fin

Tilting Shaft

Starboard Fin

Servo Power Unit

Main Power Unit

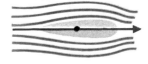
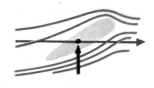
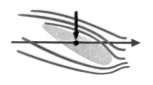

Above: How a stabilizer system controls the fins which reduce a ship's rolling. The servo power unit controls the main power unit. Below: The effects of the fins – top, fin level, no effect; middle, fin angled up provides upward lift; bottom, fin angled down exerts downward force. Thus if the ship starts a roll to starboard, the starboard fin is angled up, the port fin down – and the roll is canceled.

Ships are usually built to order. The shipping company works out what it wants – what speed, what capacity, roughly what size, what type of engines, and so on. The designer then sets to work, taking a similar existing ship as his starting point. Plans are drawn and a model made and tested.

The hull of a ship is in fact a huge and complex girder, designed to withstand all kinds of stresses at sea. The worst of these occur when a ship meets waves head on. As it rides across the crest of a wave, bow and stern are unsupported and tend to droop – this is called hogging. When bow and stern are on crests the middle is unsupported and tends to sag. A ship heading into waves may pitch up over one wave and slam down into the next. This causes enormous stresses, probably submerging the bows.

When waves reach a ship from the side it rolls. Every vessel has its own rolling time, just as a pendulum has its swinging time. If the rhythm of the waves happens to match that of the ship the roll builds up and rapidly gets out of hand. The captain must alter course into the wind to stop the roll. However, designers have largely overcome this problem by fitting stabilizers. Hinged fins stick out from the hull well below the water line. They are controlled by sensitive gyroscopes which detect the speed and degree of the roll

and adjust both fins to correct it. Another much simpler and cheaper stabilizer sometimes used consists of a pair of water tanks, one at each side of the ship, connected by a pipe. The system is designed so that when the ship heels to port the water is in the starboard tank, where it counters the roll; and by the time the ship rolls to starboard the water has crossed back to counter the new roll.

Scientists test experimental models in wave tanks to assess their behavior in heavy seas. They also test each new model to see that it slips through the water with as little resistance as possible, and to check on the amount of wave it makes at different speeds. As a ship speeds up it makes larger waves, and so wastes more power. For every ship there is a best possible speed – going any faster wastes too much fuel in wave-making to be worth while.

Six of the basic hull forms. At the top is the flush-decked ship. Second is the three-island ship, in which forecastle, bridge and poop are all parts of the hull. Number three has forecastle only, number four a forecastle and poop, number five a combined forecastle and bridge. The sixth has a raised quarter deck.

The Birth of a Ship

Computers, welding and giant cranes have brought many changes to shipbuilding.

Above: Two stages in the making of a supertanker.

Always a big event. A vessel slides gracefully into the water.

Shipyards use the most modern methods of preparing and handling the materials needed for building ships. For cutting out intricately shaped steel plates, flame cutters are guided by an electronic control unit which automatically follows the outlines on a scale drawing. Measurements from the plans are fed into a computer which works out the path of the cutter or the drafting pen. The same method can be used to operate giant presses which bend steel plates into shape. But for rounding out the curves of the hull the old methods are still used. To make the right curves, lengths of soft iron are bent to shape.

Whole sections of the hull are put together in the assembly shop, lifted out to the berth and positioned by powerful cranes. Finally they are welded to neighboring units. This is much quicker than the old method of cutting out each plate and riveting it on individually. Welding is also neater and stronger than riveting, and much of it can be done automatically, especially in building up each unit before it is brought to the ship.

Once the hull is complete, engines and other machinery are lowered into place. The superstructure is added, and electricians, plumbers, shipwrights, carpenters and painters fit out the ship — though if it is to be launched on a slipway all this must wait until the ship is afloat.

Hundreds of years ago, ships were often built in an inlet off a river. This inlet might be either natural or specially dug. At low tide, when the inlet was dry, workmen built a dam to keep the water out. The ship was then built in the inlet, which was really a dry dock. When it was finished the dam was knocked down at low tide so that as the tide rose the ship could be floated out.

Then a new method was developed; ships were built on a sloping slipway on the foreshore. Once the hull is complete and has had several coats of paint it is ready for launching, stern first. The scaffolding is taken down, the sliding ways are greased, the wedges that hold the ship are removed, and the hull slides down the slipway into the water. The tide must be just right. If the water level is only a few inches too high, the stern would lift up while the rest of the hull was still on the slipway, and the hull might bend. If the water level is too low, the stern might droop, bending the hull the other way. And of course the longer the ship the greater the problems and dangers at launching time. For this reason many shipbuilders are now turning back to the old method of building ships in a dry dock, especially for very long ships like supertankers. But dry docks are expensive, and another answer to the problem of getting large ships into the water is to build them in two sections. Each half is launched separately and they are joined together when they are afloat.

Supported by a maze of scaffolding, a new ship takes shape in the shipyard.

Stars and Sextants

Slowly and painfully the early seafarers learned to navigate when out of sight of land.

When early seafarers sailed out of sight of land, how did they know where they were, or which way to set their course? The answer is that at first they did not know. In time they discovered certain helpful facts – for example, that clouds often form over islands. From this they could guess that because there was often a cloud in a certain direction there was probably land below it. And in time they worked out various aids, such as the sounding pole or line, and the idea of carrying birds. When these birds were released they would fly toward the nearest land.

An early mariner's compass

Below: The traverse board, an aid to finding a ship's position. The helmsman inserted pegs to show how many half-hour periods the ship sailed in any direction. Estimated speed was entered in the four rows of holes at the foot of the board. At the end of each watch the ship's progress was worked out from the information on the board.

The backstaff, an early instrument for measuring the height of the sun. Looking along the main cross-beam, the navigator sighted the horizon through the slit. He then moved the sliding piece on the upper curved arm until the sun's shadow fell on the horizon slit, and read the height off the scale.

Then of course there was the sun. Since the sun rose in the east and set in the west, other directions could be roughly worked out from the sun's height (altitude) above the horizon.

For sailing at night, ancient seafarers learned to use the stars as a guide. They noticed that the star Kochab was steady in the sky at near enough due north. They also saw that the Great Bear circled Kochab, and that whereas when seen from the Nile Delta it just touched the horizon at its lowest point, the further north one went the higher off the sea it was. In other words, they had learned to work out how far north or south they were by measuring the altitude of a star (its angle above the horizon).

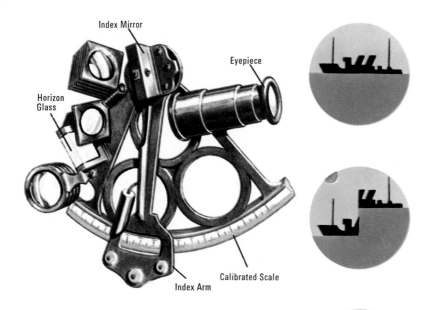

Index Mirror

Eyepiece

Horizon Glass

Calibrated Scale

Index Arm

Above: The sextant. The navigator sights the horizon through the eyepiece – right, top. He then moves the index arm (with the index mirror) until he also sees the sun, reflected by the index mirror on to the horizon glass – middle. He adjusts the image of the sun, by moving the index arm, until it "sits" on the horizon – bottom. He then reads the sun's altitude off the calibrated arm of the sextant.

Below: Finding a ship's position with a sextant. The navigator selects a star. Then he finds from printed tables the point on earth where the star is directly overhead. He marks this "substellar point" on the map. He then uses his sextant to find what angle, from his position, the star is from the zenith. (The zenith is the point in the heavens directly overhead). The navigator knows that each degree of angle represents 60 sea miles from the substellar point. So if the angle on the sextant is 30°, he knows his ship is 30 × 60 = 1800 sea miles from the substellar point.

He draws a circle on his map, with its center at the substellar point, and with a radius of 1800 sea miles (large circle, bottom diagram). He now repeats the whole process with another star, and draws a second circle. Now he knows that his ship is at one of the two places where the circles join. These two places may be hundreds of miles apart, so he needs only a very rough idea of his position to know which is the right one.

It was not until the invention of the chronometer (a very accurate clock) in the eighteenth century that seafarers were able to find their position with any accuracy.

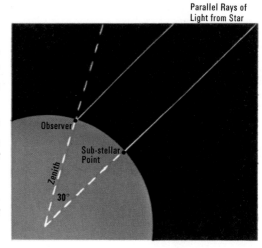

Parallel Rays of Light from Star

Observer

Sub-stellar Point

Zenith

30°

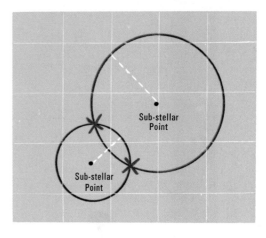

Sub-stellar Point

Sub-stellar Point

Today seamen use a sextant to find the altitude of the sun and stars. Seamen of the ancient world probably held their arm outstretched and noted how many fingers-breadth the star was above the horizon.

An ancient astronomer called Ptolemy was the first to divide the map of the world with lines of latitude and longitude. Lines of latitude run round the earth parallel to the equator. Lines of longitude run north and south round the earth from pole to pole. Sailors could now describe their position at sea as so many degrees of latitude north or south of the equator, and so many degrees of longitude east or west of some given point.

But there was no way of finding a ship's longitude, even if the sun or stars could be seen. (If the sky was overcast there was no way of finding latitude either.) Dead reckoning gave a rough idea of a ship's position. This was a way of finding the position by guessing the ship's speed through the water and using an hour glass to tell the time traveled.

The first improvement on dead reckoning did not appear until the sixteenth century. It was known as the log-line. This was a piece of wood attached to a line with equally spaced knots in it. A man threw the log overboard and counted the number of knots slipping through his fingers in one minute – timed with a sand glass. If the seaman counted five knots, the ship was said to be traveling at five knots (five nautical miles per hour).

Modern Navigation

Ships still carry sextant, chronometer and magnetic compass, but navigation today relies more on electronics than on the stars.

A typical layout of the instruments in the ship's wheelhouse, with everything set out in one large console.

BOW THRUSTERS

Steering a large ship at slow speed is very difficult. The rudder has little effect – the ship responds sluggishly. The bow (or side) thruster helps to solve this problem. Below the waterline, near the bows, a tunnel passes through the ship from one side to the other. It is open at both ends. In the middle of the tunnel is a propeller which can thrust water out of one side or the other. When the ship is moving slowly, the thrust of water pushes the bows round effectively.

Once clear of port and congested coastal waters, the captain of a modern liner sets his course and leaves the automatic pilot to steer the ship. The slightest change in course is noticed by the gyrocompass and passed on to the automatic pilot, which alters the setting of the rudder. Meanwhile an electronic log keeps a continuous record of speed and direction; ultrasonic depth-sounding (sonar) equipment measures and records the depth of the sea bed; automatic direction-finding equipment receives signals from shore transmitters and plots the ship's course; radar screens pick out any other ships in the vicinity; and officers in the radio room are in constant contact with the shore, and with other ships. There are regular weather, wave and ice reports. It is usual to follow a route based on the most favorable wind and wave conditions, rather than on the shortest distance.

Direction-finding was originally a matter of tuning in to a signal transmitted from a known point (marked on a chart) with a highly directional antenna – two or more such bearings enable the navigator to fix his position. Today's systems rely on instruments

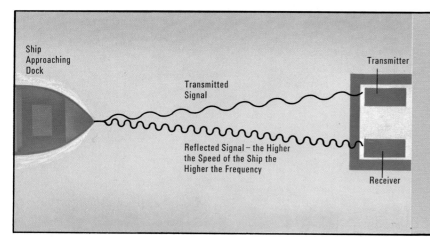

When a fast aircraft flies overhead, the pitch (frequency) of its scream sounds higher as it approaches than when it goes away from us. This is known as the Doppler effect, and it is applied both in radar and in sonar, as well as in navigation by satellite. A Doppler radar installation on the shore can be used to measure the exact speed of an approaching ship – see diagram. If two installations are used, one aimed at the bow and one at the stern, changes in the ship's course can be measured as well.

DEAD RECKONING TODAY

Some ships carry computers which calculate their position by using signals received from satellites. But not all ships are equipped with these navigational aids and dead reckoning is still used. In fact one of the most advanced aids relies on it – on the principle that if a ship's speed and changes in course can be measured accurately, then its precise progress (and therefore its position) can be calculated. This system was used for navigating nuclear submarines *Nautilus* and *Skate* under the polar ice cap in 1958.

A special "collision avoidance system" radar unit. It shows the course of the ship in relation to those of other ships, and "advises" the navigator what (if any) avoiding action he should take to prevent any danger of collision.

Below: The view from the bridge of a large tanker. The ship stretches a long way ahead, giving some idea of the problems of steering giant vessels.

which compare the times taken by signals from two or more stations to reach the ship.

Radar, on the other hand, involves sending out pulses of radio waves with a directional antenna, and receiving the echoes of these pulses, which are reflected back by any objects in their path. As radio waves travel at a constant speed, not only the direction but also the distance of objects can be calculated. Thus, when visibility is poor, the captain can "see" and keep track of other ships in the area. Near land the radar screen shows the shape of the coastline – from which he can identify his position. Advanced radar systems can plot and show the course of other ships, they can also show the effect of changing one's own course, which can be helpful in avoiding a collision.

Sonar uses the same principle as radar, but with pulses of sound. The latest development gives the captain a further means of checking his position, using computers and electronic "maps" of the sea bed. Continuous readings from the ship's sonar are passed to the computer, which can then pinpoint the ship's position on the electronic map.

A B C
D E F G
H I J K
L M N O
P Q R S
T U V W
X Y Z

1 2
3 4
5 6
7 8
9 0

Rules of the Sea

An elaborate code of warning signs and international regulations helps to ensure a safe passage for every ship.

If two ships are approaching each other on a collision course, they must both alter direction to starboard (right). If their courses are crossing, the ship which has the other on the starboard side must get out of the way. When maneuvering to avoid a collision, both ships must use their sirens to tell the other what they are doing – one short blast means "I am altering course to starboard"; two short blasts, "I am altering course to port"; three "My engines are going astern". These three signals represent the letters "e", "i" and "s" in the Morse Code. Another method of signaling is with flags, using the International Code of Signals (illustrated – left).

All ships have to carry lights at night – a red one on the port side, a green one on the starboard, and white lights at the stern (not visible from ahead) and on the mastheads (not visible from astern).

Buoys are anchored in the water to guide shipping, especially in coastal waters and estuaries, and in very busy seaways. Some buoys mark the limits of deep-water channels, others warn of hidden rocks, shoals or wrecks. All buoys are marked on charts, so by studying his chart in advance the navigator knows what to look out for. The chart also indicates prominent landmarks; high and low water lines and details of tides in harbors; the depth of water, and whether the sea bed is sand or rock.

When a ship nears port the captain will usually call for a pilot to navigate his ship along the final stretch, especially if it is through difficult and busy waters. The pilot knows local conditions and problems much better than a ship's captain, calling at many ports all over the world, could ever do.

Above: Each flag, as well as representing a letter of the alphabet, has its own special meaning. For example: B, "I am carrying dangerous goods"; C, "Yes"; D, "Keep clear"; G, "I want a pilot"; L, "You should stop at once"; N, "No"; O, "Man overboard"; P – the Blue Peter – "I am about to sail"; Q, "Quarantine"; V, "I need help".

Navigation lights: Top left, the two white lights shown when at anchor. The remaining five pictures show the lights carried by a moving ship – white on fore and main masts (and at the stern), green on the starboard side and red on the port. By observing the positions of these lights, sailors can tell the course of another ship even in total darkness.

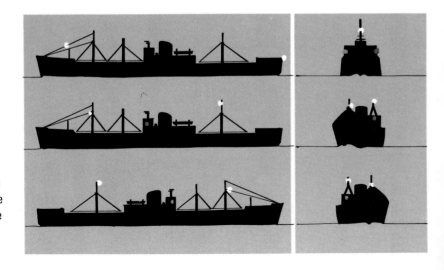

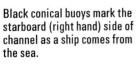

Black conical buoys mark the starboard (right hand) side of a channel as a ship comes from the sea.

Red can-shaped buoys mark the port (left hand) side of a channel.

Shallow water dividing a channel is marked by buoys like the one on the right. The markings vary according to whether the main channel is to the right or left of the buoy.

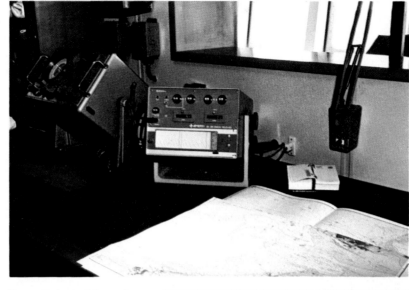

Above: A chart of the waters at the entrance to a harbor and navigational aids in the chartroom of a modern vessel.

Green buoys mark a wreck. A cone-shaped one should be kept to starboard, a can-shaped one to port.

Yellow buoys mark quarantine anchoring grounds for ships with infectious disease on board.

Buoys like this mark shallow water in the open sea.

With their powerful light systems, radio beacons and sound signals, lighthouses are another of the signposts of the sea. Today the world's tallest lighthouse has a 348-foot steel tower. Its light is visible for 20 miles. The lighthouse is near Yokohama in Japan (below). Many lighthouses are built on headlands, but others are needed out at sea – as at Buzzards Bay, Massachusetts (right).

Buoys like this mark the middle of a main channel.

Sinking and Salvage

Despite safety precautions and modern equipment, about 15 ships sink every month, and there are 500 or so lesser casualties.

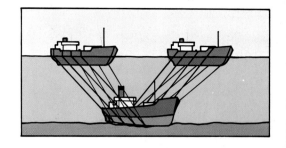

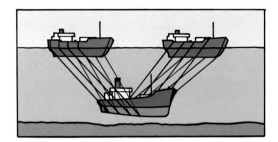

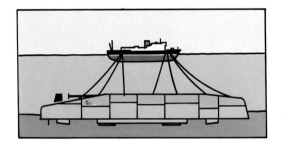

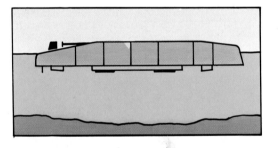

"Abandoned in sinking condition in stormy weather, all life feared lost, air search conducted, vessel presumed sunk – Broke in two in heavy seas and sank – Sank after cargo shifted in heavy swell – Ran aground, engine room and all holds flooded, partly submerged and back broken amidships – Sent out distress signal the day after leaving port, air search found no trace of vessel or survivors – Collision, followed by fire which spread rapidly, abandoned, exploded, and sank – Overdue, no signals received, no trace

Sunken ships are often raised as shown in the top pair of diagrams. Cables are passed under the ship and attached to two salvage vessels. At low tide all slack in the cables is taken up. The salvage vessels rise with the tide, lifting the sunken ship off the sea bed. If all openings in the wreck can be sealed, compressed air is pumped into the wreck itself (lower pair of diagrams).

Left: Wrecks sunk in the Goodwin Sands, a treacherous range of sandbanks in the Strait of Dover, England, visible only at low tide.

Below: An artist's impression of a shipwreck. This painting by J. M. W. Turner, dates from about 1805.

found – Struck submerged object, extensive bottom damage, temporary repairs carried out, returned to port – Fire after explosion in hold – Engine room fire". These are a selection of casualties at sea reported during a typical month.

The most common causes of total losses are fires, explosions, running aground in fog, and sinking in heavy seas. Partial losses – accidents in which the ship is not completely lost – are most often caused by damage to machinery and collisions.

The captain of a ship in danger of sinking immediately sends out a distress signal, reporting his position, and what is wrong. Nearby vessels, if there are any,

Above: The tanker "Igara" ran aground off Singapore. Unable to free the forward section, the salvors used explosives to break the ship in two. They then refloated the after half (photograph) and towed it to Japan. There a new forward half was built on, and the ship was put back into service.

Right: The tanker "Torrey Canyon" breaking up in 1967.

AUTOMATIC RESCUE ALERT SYSTEMS

Most merchant ships are supposed to report their positions every few days. The US coastguards run an Automatic Merchant Vessel Reporting system (AMVER) – ships report their position regularly and a computer plots and records their course. A new satellite system, Global Rescue Alerting Network (GRAN) is being developed. With it a device on the ship automatically sends out a signal in the event of a disaster. This should make it impossible for ships simply to disappear.

will hurry to the scene, and coastguard stations send out aircraft and helicopters. Lifeboats are also sent out if the ship in distress is close enough to land. Sometimes they arrive in time, sometimes not. On many occasions the weather conditions are so bad that even if the search aircraft flew right over the ship, it might not be seen.

If the accident is less severe and there is no danger of sinking, the captain will radio for assistance, and ocean-going salvage tugs will be sent to help. These tugs carry powerful pumps (for putting out fires, or pumping out flooded ships), divers and diving gear, underwater cutting and welding apparatus and patching materials. Their job is to patch up the ship if necessary, and tow it to port. They are stationed throughout the world at main points on important shipping routes.

Round Ships and Long Ships

By trial and error seagoing craft improved from the Stone Age dug-out to the long ships of the Phoenicians.

thick rope fixed down at bow and stern and passing along the middle of the ship over a row of crutches. It looked crude, but it worked. The truss prevented bow and stern drooping (hogging) when the ship rode up on a wave.

The ancient Phoenicians were among the most famous of early seafarers. Their homeland was a narrow strip of infertile land sandwiched between the Mediterranean Sea and the desert. So it was not surprising that they turned to the sea for their living. Phoenician seamen were probably the first ever to sail deliberately out of sight of land, and the first ever to sail round Africa (the voyage, in around 600 BC, took three years). Their trading ships were the merchantmen of the Mediterranean. They sailed as far as Britain in the north.

The Phoenicians built quite different types of ships for trading and for fighting. Round ships, powered by sail with oars as a standby, were used for commerce (no records have been found to show what they looked like). Long ships, sleek and fast, powered by oars with sail as an auxiliary, were used for

Seafarers of the ancient world were their own designers and shipbuilders. They were constantly trying to improve their ships. And they came up with some very good ideas.

The Brigg boat, a dug-out dating back to the Stone Age, was 48 feet long and four feet six inches wide, which for a dug-out was enormous. To increase its strength the maker had wedged cross-pieces of timber at intervals along the boat, bored a series of holes along each side, and lashed thongs of rawhide across the boat and through the holes. This would have held the sides of the dug-out firmly against the crosspieces.

To improve lengthwise strength, the ancient Egyptians invented the truss – a

Above: Craft like these have been used on Lake Titicaca in Peru since ancient times. Known as balsas, they are made of bundles of reeds. These boats last only for a few months, as the reeds soon rot and fall to pieces.

fighting. The Phoenicians probably invented the bireme and trireme – war galleys in which the oars and oarsmen were banked up on two (bi-) or three (tri-) levels. This gave greater speed without increasing length. The hull was often extended at the bow to form a pointed ram – the ship's main armament.

The Vikings are probably the most famous of ancient seafarers. They sailed across the Atlantic to North America. Their ships were long, fast, and very seaworthy. This was proved when an exact replica of one of these early long-boats was sailed across the Atlantic in 1893.

A long ship and a round ship from ancient Greece, about 500 BC – from a vase found at Vulci.

An ancient Egyptian boat of about 2900 BC, with a truss to prevent hogging. The three oars on either side of the stern were for steering. The hull was made of short brick-like blocks of wood pegged together. Such a ship could not have survived for long in heavy seas.

Voyages of Discovery

More changes were made to maps of the world between 1475 and 1525 than had been made in the previous 1000 years.

Above: Christopher Columbus

A map of the world printed in 1486. It is based on the world map prepared by the astronomer Ptolemy in the second century AD. America had not yet been discovered and nobody knew how far South Africa extended.

Many centuries passed before any real advances were made on the ships of the Phoenicians and Vikings. But by the time of the great voyages of discovery, some progress had taken place. Ships now had several masts, and carried a variety of sails. They had more complex rigging, which meant that they were easier to control. They had a modern-style rudder controlled by a wheel. They were built longer and deeper, which gave them more space inside and a better grip in the water.

With the capture of Constantinople in 1453 the Moslems completed their conquest of the eastern Mediterranean. This forced the rulers of Christian Europe, who depended for their revenues on the eastern trade, to look for new routes to their old markets. Prince Henry of Por-

tugal devoted his life to the search for a sea route round Africa to the East.

In 1486–87, 27 years after Henry the Navigator's death, his dream was finally realized by Bartholomeo Diaz. The first part of the voyage, round the bulge of West Africa, was by now almost routine. But south of Walfish Bay strong winds blew Diaz's ship away from the security of land and out into northerly gales. These gales blew them south for 13 days, after which the wind slackened and Diaz headed east, expecting to reach the African coast. When after three days they had still not sighted land, they must have feared themselves lost for ever. Then Diaz had an idea. He altered course to the north – and it was not long before they sighted land. Diaz had indeed discovered the southern tip of Africa. His successor Vasco da Gama completed the voyage up Africa's eastern coast and across to India.

While the Portuguese were searching for a way to the East round Africa, the Spaniards dreamed of reaching the East by sailing west. Nobody knew about the American continent, so that in theory if

Below: Upper – Columbus' first voyage, 1492. He made three further voyages. Lower – Vasco da Gama's voyage of discovery round Africa to India, 1497–99.

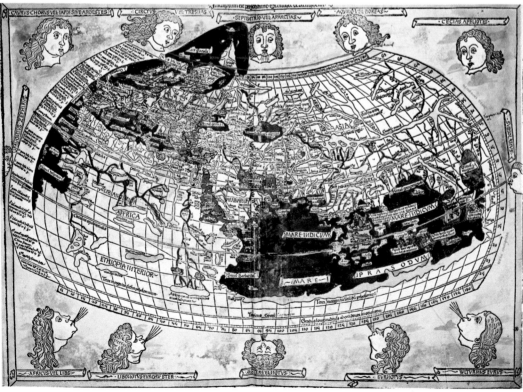

one sailed west one's first landfall would be the eastern coast of Asia. On 3 August 1492 Christopher Columbus set off on his famous voyage.

After a quick and uneventful crossing of 36 days he reached the islands now called the Bahamas. From there he sailed on to discover Cuba and Hispaniola. Columbus was one of the great discoverers, but he was no scientist. He was so wrapped up in his theories that he was convinced he had reached eastern Asia. It was left to Amerigo Vespucci to realize that they had discovered a New World.

The maps of the world were redrawn to include the new continent (or as much of it as was known). The discoverers turned their attention to reaching the East by sailing round America – to the south, and to the north-west.

The north-west passage occupied such well-known seafarers as John and Sebastian Cabot, Martin Frobisher and others for many years. They discovered Nova, Scotia, Newfoundland, Canada. They found excellent fishing grounds – but

cold and ice defeated their attempts at any north-west passage.

On 20 September 1519 the Portuguese navigator Ferdinand Magellan set sail with five ships and 234 men to search for a passage round South America.

On 21 October 1520 the expedition rounded a headland and saw a channel running westwards. Hopefully they followed it. After 38 days of nerve-wracking navigation through channels which were often narrow, they sailed out into open sea. This sea, where no ship had ever sailed before, Magellan named the Pacific (the peaceful). The straits through which he had passed became the Straits of Magellan. The expedition pressed on to the Mariana Islands and the Philippines, where – in a fight with the natives – Magellan was killed. What remained of the expedition continued westwards, at last reaching Spain on 6 September 1522. It had taken three years, and they returned with only 18 men and one ship, but they had sailed right round the world.

After battling through stormy seas for almost one month, the Portuguese navigator Ferdinand Magellan rounded Cape Horn and sailed into the calm waters of an ocean he named the Pacific.

A map of the world printed in 1570. Diaz had sailed round Africa; da Gama had continued to India; Columbus, Vespucci and Magellan had put America on the map. The voyages of discovery had at last given the known world a more accurate shape.

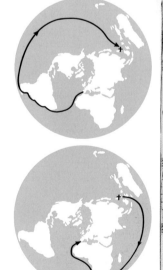

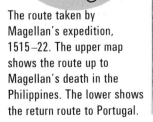

The route taken by Magellan's expedition, 1515–22. The upper map shows the route up to Magellan's death in the Philippines. The lower shows the return route to Portugal.

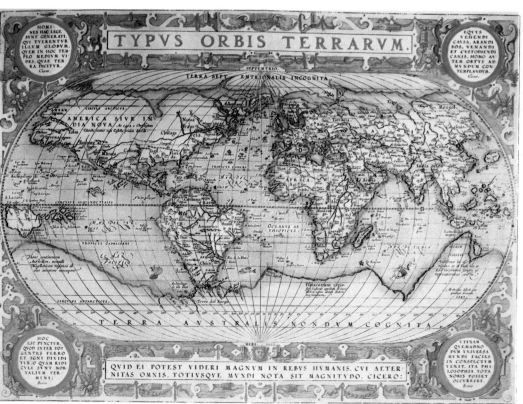

TYPVS ORBIS TERRARVM.

Great Days of Sail

As competition for the China tea trade grew, the slow but sturdy tea wagons gave way to the clippers — craft designed for speed at the expense of cargo capacity.

Above: The forward progress of a ship sailing into the wind has increased greatly over the centuries. A Viking longship could sail only a few degrees into the wind. The angle for a modern yacht is up to 45°.

Above: The windjammer "Preussen", the only five-masted fully-rigged ship ever built. The total area of her 47 sails was well over an acre.

For hundreds of years after the voyages of discovery the sailing ship slowly changed. Ship designers made ships less top-heavy by cutting down the towering castles at bow and stern; they strengthened the hull; they built larger ships; and they built a lot more of them. The new ships were needed to cope with the ever increasing trade (and wars) between nations, and to carry colonists and slaves. But the ships were tubby and slow — little more than improved versions of those sailed by Columbus and Magellan.

Then there were two important changes. First, the Americans started building for speed, to beat British warships in the War of Independence. The Baltimore clippers were small, sleek, and fast. Secondly, in 1832 the British government canceled the East India Company's monopoly over the China tea trade. With the China tea trade in mind, and the Baltimore clippers as his starting point, John Griffith of New York designed a new kind of ocean-going merchant ship, the *Rainbow*. Launched in 1845, she was the first of the great Yankee clippers.

Low in the water, with layer upon layer of sails, the Yankee

East Indiamen like this were sturdy, and almost as well armed as warships. But basically they were very similar to the ships of the Spanish Armada some 200 years earlier. Known as Tea Wagons, they were slow, with a top speed of only 9 or 10 knots. This did not worry the East India Company. They had no competitors in the tea trade and were making good profits. But with the end of their monopoly and the start of the race to China, the Wagons gave way to the new Clippers.

Above: A ship's figurehead was often elaborately carved and richly gilded.

Right: The "Herzogin Cecilie", one of the fastest windjammers. Launched in 1902, she was built for the North Atlantic passenger trade. Later she earned a good living as a cargo ship until she was wrecked in 1936.

CLIPPERS AND WINDJAMMERS
The clippers were sensitive ships. Captains would supervise loading to ensure that their vessel was properly balanced in the water. At sea lengths of heavy chain were moved about the deck to balance the ship. Expertly handled they were very fast. But a large crew was needed to drive a clipper fast day and night. The windjammers, with a much smaller crew and more cargo, could still carry sail under gale conditions which would have wrecked a clipper. Under such conditions they could equal the speed of any clipper.

clippers were designed for speed at the expense of strength, capacity, and long life. Unlike all previous sailing ships, whose rounded bows lifted them over the waves, the clippers sliced through them. They reached speeds of over 20 knots, and on many occasions covered well over 400 nautical miles in 24 hours sailing.

Immediately the China tea trade became a race to see who could get each season's tea back first. Other races followed, for gold – to California in 1848–49, and to Australia in 1854. Then, in the 1860s, the railroad across the U.S. to California was completed, and the opening of the Suez Canal gave steam ships the advantage in the tea race. The clipper's brief moment of glory was over.

But steamships needed a chain of coaling stations, whereas with a coop full of chickens and a supply of salt beef, sailing ships could stay at sea for months. Speed was no longer so important, cheapness was vital, and a new kind of ship appeared, the huge windjammer. With fuller hulls than the clippers, and a tougher build (most of them were made of steel), they could carry much more cargo and needed a smaller crew. Some of these "tall ships" are still afloat. They take part in the occasional race, but more often they are used as training ships for sea cadets.

Fully Rigged Clipper

With all sails set these graceful ships could "ghost" along in the lightest breeze, a pyramid of canvas towering above the sleek hull.

The Names of the Sails
1 Fore royal. 2 Fore topgallant. 3 Fore upper topsail. 4 Fore lower topsail. 5 Fore course. 6 Flying jib. 7 Jib. 8 Fore topmast staysail. 9 Main royal. 10 Main topgallant. 11 Main royal staysail. 12 Main upper topsail. 13 Main lower topsail. 14 Main topgallant staysail. 15 Main course. 16 Main topmast staysail. 17 Mizzen royal. 18 Mizzen topgallant. 19 Mizzen upper topsail. 20 Mizzen topgallant staysail. 21 Mizzen lower topsail. 22 Mizzen topmast staysail. 23 Mizzen course. 24 Spencer. 25 Spanker.

Other sails were sometimes carried, but these are not shown in the picture. One ship, the East Indiaman *Essex*, carried a total of 63 sails.

The three masts are (bow to stern) fore, main and mizzen (most sails take their names from the mast, and their position on the mast – starting with the course, and going up to the royal). The cross spars from which the square sails hang are yards. The spars from which spanker and spencer hang are gaffs. Those at the foot of these two fore-and-aft sails are booms. The crosstrees (one to each mast) are level with the bottoms of the topgallants. The platforms two sails lower are the tops (fore top, main top and mizzen top). Each mast is in fact named in three parts: the lowest section, up to the "top", is simply the mast; next comes the topmast, from top to cross trees; and finally the topgallant mast.

Birth of the Steamship

For centuries men had dreamed of making ships that would travel against wind and current. The steam engine made this dream come true.

In 1705 Thomas Newcomen built the first steam engine. Thirty years later an English clock-repairer built a steamship powered by a Newcomen engine joined to a pair of paddle wheels. It failed. The engine was single-acting (it could push but not pull).

In 1783 the Marquis Claude de Jouffroy built a two-cylinder steam engine (one cylinder to push, the other to pull). It was linked to twin paddle wheels. The engine was fitted into his *Pyroscaphe*, which became the first steam-powered vessel to move against the current – on the Saône River in France. But Jouffroy ran out of money, and it was left to John Fitch to start the world's first regular steamboat service in 1790. It ran between Philadelphia and Trenton on the Delaware River. Fitch's boat was driven by stern paddles, and was powered by an improved steam engine. Unfortunately Fitch chose a route which was well served by stagecoach. Lack of passengers forced him to give up.

Meanwhile, the Scottish engineer James Watt had invented his famous steam en-

FULTON'S STEAMBOATS

The American inventor Robert Fulton (1765–1815) started his working life as a painter, but gave up art for engineering in 1793. While in Paris, the U.S. Minister to France offered to assist Fulton in building a steamboat. This boat was launched in the Seine in 1803, but the French were not impressed. The American government now offered Fulton $15,000 to develop a steamboat, and the *Clermont* was launched in the East river in 1807. It weighed 150 tons, measured 120 feet from stem to stern and had a 30-foot funnel. The boat was a great success on the Hudson river.

Above "Charlotte Dundas", built in 1801 to tow barges on Scotland's Forth and Clyde Canal. It was the first practical steamboat. "Charlotte Dundas" (which was powered by James Watt's new type of steam engine) was sturdy and efficient. She towed two 70-ton barges 19½ miles in six hours against a strong headwind.

Left: Robert Fulton's "North River Steamboat of Clermont", the world's first steamboat to run at a profit. She is seen here in her final form with an enclosed cabin (1807).

gine. It was far more efficient than previous engines, and another Scot, William Symington, adapted Watt's invention for powering a ship. His *Charlotte Dundas* proved a complete success. Propelled by a single paddle-wheel at the stern, it towed barges along the Forth-Clyde Canal in the years 1801–02. But it was withdrawn from service after complaints that its wash was damaging the canal banks. However, the steamship had proved its worth, and within a few years Robert Fulton's *Clermont* and John Stevens' *Phoenix* began regular services on the Hudson and Delaware Rivers.

The next thirty years saw few advances, except in size. The *Great Western* (1837), the first steamship designed to cross the Atlantic, was powered by engines similar to those of the *Clermont*. It was propelled by side-paddles, and built of wood.

There followed a period of rapid advance. Designers began to use metal hulls, screw propellers and better steam engines. The first iron ship was built in 1821. But it was another twenty years or so before it was realized that metal ships were cheaper, lighter and stronger than wooden ones.

Above: "Sirus" (left center), the first ship to cross the Atlantic under steam power, and her rival, Brunel's "Great Western" (center), in New York harbor after their historic race in April 1838. "Great Western" arrived four hours behind, but as she started four days after "Sirius" she made the faster crossing.

A steam turbine is simple and efficient. The vanes fitted round the shaft are turned by a jet of steam and drive the screw through a series of gears.

ENGINES AND PROPELLERS

SS stands for steam ship, MS for motor ship. Steam ships are powered by steam turbines, motor ships by diesel engines. Both use oil as fuel, though until around 1930 steam turbines were run on coal. Diesel engines have several advantages over steam turbines: they use less fuel; they are smaller; and there is no delay while the ship builds up steam.

Whichever type of engine is used, it is coupled to the propeller through gears. Most engines are at their most efficient at fairly high speeds, while the best speed for the propeller is below 100 revolutions per minute. It is usual to couple several engines to the same propeller. This allows one engine to be stopped for servicing without the ship having to stop.

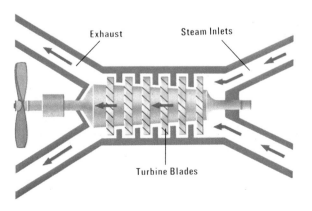

Exhaust   Steam Inlets

Turbine Blades

The Atlantic Ferry

Above: The graceful lines of the "France", the longest passenger liner ever built (1035 feet).

Fierce competition for the Atlantic speed record led to a series of triumphs – and one tragedy.

In 1838 *Great Western* and *Sirius* raced each other across the Atlantic. They proved that steamships could make the voyage. Two years later the Cunard Line was founded to ply a regular mail and passenger service. The race to provide the fastest trans-Atlantic ferry was on. The ship which made the fastest crossing claimed the title of Blue Riband of the Atlantic. As late as 1867 this was held by a paddle-steamer, the *Scotia*. But in that year the title was won by the screw-driven SS *City of Paris*.

The next major advance was the development of the steam turbine – smaller, lighter, and less complex than the massive steam engines. Cunard decided on turbines for their *Lusitania* and for her sister ship the *Mauretania*, the most famous of all the old Atlantic liners. *Mauretania* won the Blue Riband in 1909, with a speed of 26.06 knots, and held it for over twenty years. The German liners *Bremen* and *Europa* and the Italian *Rex* fought over the Blue Riband for a few years, and then it was the turn of the French *Normandie* and the Cunard *Queen Mary*. Both ships set new standards of design and comfort. In 1938 the *Queen Mary* finally won, with a speed of 31.69 knots, and it was not until 1952 that she lost the Blue Riband to the *United States*, which pushed the speed up to over 35 knots. After this the battle for the Blue Riband was over – the place of the fast Atlantic ferryboat has been taken over by aircraft.

Above, top: The "Mauretania". In her day she was the largest ship ever built. She captured the Blue Riband in 1909 with an average speed of 20.06 knots – and held it for over 20 years. Above: The "United States", the world's fastest-ever liner with a top speed of 41.75 knots. She won the Blue Riband in 1952.

The Titanic Disaster

No effort was spared in the race across the Atlantic, and every luxury was built into the *Titanic*. The largest ship afloat, she had nine decks, and her boilers burned 40 tons of coal an hour. Her owners claimed that she was unsinkable. After trials early in 1912 they sent her on her maiden voyage across the Atlantic to win the Blue Riband. The voyage was widely advertised and the *Titanic* carried 2206 passengers.

At 11.46 pm ship's time on 14 April 1912 the ship struck an iceberg. The blow tore a gash in the hull almost the length of the ship, and less than three hours later the *Titanic* sank. Over 1500 people died in the disaster, which was the worst in history. There were not enough lifeboats, and there had been no lifeboat drill.

Following the disaster there was an enquiry, and from that time on all passenger liners had to carry enough lifeboats. Passengers had to be instructed in their use, and standards were worked out to make ships safer. The practice of dividing the hull into watertight compartments was an old one. But before the *Titanic* disaster no one had worked out how much division was needed to make a ship safe.

CAVITATION

A screw that turns too fast churns up the water, creating hollows and bubbles. This is called cavitation and wastes power. Because the *Mauretania*'s turbines were linked to the screws by direct drive they had to run at a speed too low for efficiency in order to cut down cavitation.

Below: The "Queen Elizabeth 2", a luxury resort hotel for holiday cruising. In the summer she runs a transatlantic service. In the winter she follows the sun. The ship's superstructure is made of aluminum. This saves weight and thus reduces the vessel's draft. It allows her to dock at small ports around the world. She cruises at 28.5 knots, but today speed is less important than comfort and economy.

Above: The sinking of the "Titanic".

■ Recreational Facilities

■ Fuel, Water, Engines

■ Cargo and Supplies

■ Restaurants and Kitchens

■ Crew Quarters

■ Passenger Accommodation and Lounges

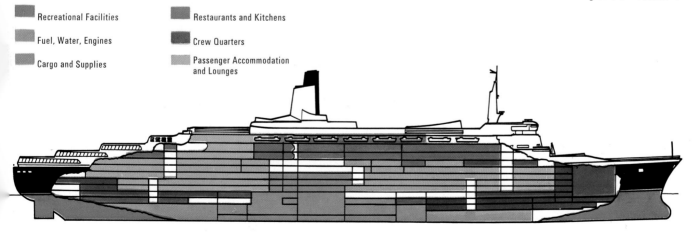

Cargo Ships

Many nations depend for their existence on the ships which bring them food from distant lands.

In the days of sail, ships arrived when they arrived. Factories were sometimes idle while they waited for the next cargo of raw materials. The docks were sometimes idle, sometimes very busy – dock workers were hired by the day. Today cargo shipping is as tightly timetabled as are air and rail services.

Wherever possible, cargo is carried in bulk, in special ships. This saves time and money, because bulk cargoes can be loaded and unloaded quickly. Biggest of all are the oil tankers. Many carry over 200,000 tons of oil, and are over 300 yards long. Yet they need a crew of only about thirty. There are bulk carriers for sugar, grain, timber, ores, chemicals, and so on. The disadvantage of special bulk ships is that they must make the return journey "in ballast" (i.e. partly filled with water for stability, but carrying no cargo). This is wasteful.

General cargo liners carry almost anything. Here too speed and ease of handling are all-important, and goods are packaged in as large units as possible. More and more general cargo is packed in standard-sized containers, and carried in special container ships. These have no interior decks or holds. The hull is divided by metal guides and racks into cells, each of which holds one container.

Left: Four old-time sailing coasters. Their job included fishing, and carrying freight from port to port round the coast. Top to bottom: an English trading ketch, a Swedish roslag jagt, a Norwegian fembøring and a Dutch hektjalk.

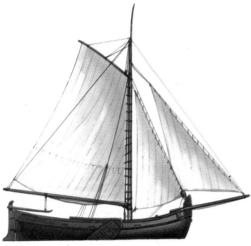

Right: A supertanker, the Japanese-built "Globtik London". With her sister ship "Globtik Tokyo" she is the world's largest ship. "Globtik London" is 1243 feet 5 inches long, 203 feet 5 inches wide, has a dead weight of 483,664 tons and a draft of 92 feet. She carries a helicopter and a crew of 38.

Below: An inland waterway barge passing through the Rhine gorge in Germany.

Right: A general cargo liner. Vessels like this normally have four or five holds and two or three decks. The ship carries its own cargo-handling gear.

FREIGHT SHIPS OF THE FUTURE
Some experts see the nuclear submarine as one of the cargo ships of the future. Deep underwater, out of reach of storms, waves and ice, ships can travel faster and at less cost than on the surface. The surface route to Japan or China is roughly twice as long as the direct route under the Arctic ice.

Right: A container ship loading and unloading (the two operations take place at the same time).

Left: "Acadia Forest", the world's first LASH ship (Lighter Aboard Ship). The traveling gantry crane in the middle of the vessel can straddle any of the 14 hatches. It can load and discharge the cargo of 73 lighters (floating containers) over the stern.

Special Purpose Ships

Safe and efficient traffic at sea would be impossible without workhorse ships, such as tugs and icebreakers.

No harbor or dock could exist without the help of the most common workhorse ship – the tug. Its main job is to push or tow large ships to and from their berth. Tugs have powerful engines – which usually take up half the hull space – and large propellers for power. Larger ocean-going tugs are used to tow almost anything almost anywhere – floating docks, crippled ships, dredgers, oil rigs, strings of barges . . .

Large ships need deep water and it is the job of dredgers to keep harbors and channels clear of mud and silt. Bucket dredgers have a continuous chain which takes the buckets down, drags them through the mud, brings them up full, and tips the mud into waiting barges. Other dredgers work like vacuum cleaners, sucking the mud up through hoses and either dumping it in the hold or squirting it well clear of the channel (see illustration below). Dredgers for use in harbors and docks are moved from place to place by tug. The one illustrated is self-powered.

Icebreakers keep open harbors, rivers and shipping routes near the poles. They clear paths through the ice for ships taking supplies to polar research stations. They have very strong, thick hulls and can steam through ice up to about three feet thick (though the Russian nuclear icebreaker, the *Lenin*, can deal with almost twice that thickness). Where the ice is very deep they use explosives, or take a run at the ice. They slide up on it with their sloping bows, and the ice breaks under the weight of the ship.

An unusual special-purpose ship, the "Flip" Research Platform. "Flip" steams along like a normal ship, and can then flip up on end, as seen in this photograph. The bow remains above water, while the remainder of the ship goes deep below the surface for underwater research.

At a steady two knots this giant dredger cuts a channel over 100 feet wide, pumping the mud well clear along its lengthy boom.

Above: A car ferry of Danish State Railways crossing between Zealand and Funen.

Below: The world's first nuclear ice-breaker, the "Lenin" (USSR) at work. The "Lenin" can operate in ice nearly six feet thick, and needs refueling only once a year.

Above: Inside one of the cable tanks on the cable ship "Mercury". The tanks can hold up to 1800 miles of cable. Exact positioning is very important in cable-laying, so cable ships must be easy to maneuver.

Above: With their powerful engines, tugs are the workhorse ships of every harbor.

Cable ships provide another vital service. They lay and repair under-sea telephone cables all over the world. They have guides and rollers at bow and stern for paying out or picking up cable, and equipment to check new cables and trace faults. These ships carry hundreds of miles of cable in huge drum-shaped holds. Special equipment is fitted to pay out cable at a constant speed and tension.

Many fishing vessels are too small to count as ships, but factory ships are rather different. Many factory trawlers are equipped to catch anything from cod to sardines, and are equally at home in tropical or polar conditions. The plant on board may produce canned fish, or blocks of frozen fish, fillets and so on.

Ports and Harbors

Special cargo ships and special berths have speeded up the work at many ports.

Top. View of a dock. In the right foreground a ship can be seen moored in a dry dock for repairs. Outside the dock area is a berth for bulk grain ships, with pipes along which the grain is sucked into silos on the shore. Above: A container berth, with gantry cranes for lifting the containers on and off the ship.

The working areas of a port, where ships load and unload, are called docks. The level of water in a dock must be fairly steady, otherwise loading would be almost impossible. If the rise and fall of the tide is more than about nine feet, enclosed docks are necessary. The water in the dock is cut off from that in the sea or river by locks. Docks always open to the sea are known as tidal docks.

Cargo Handling

Unloading a general cargo liner is a difficult operation. Long before the ship arrives the dock authorities will have received a list of its cargo. They will decide which goods will be taken straight to waiting trucks or trains, and which can be unloaded over the ship's side into barges or small coasters. Fragile items of cargo may need to be handled by themselves, but most are grouped into sets, either in a net or sling, or on pallets. Pallets are wooden platforms which can be moved by forklift truck and lifted by crane.

The authorities reserve a berth, and ensure that when the ship docks the men and equipment needed are there. Areas on the warehouse floors are marked out for long-term storage. Arrangements are made with the transport companies so that they do not all arrive at once. To unload a general cargo liner may take as long as two weeks. A container ship can be unloaded and loaded in less than 48 hours.

Handling bulk cargo at a special berth is straightforward. The equipment is always there and the storage facilities are built for that kind of cargo. There may be storage tanks into which bulk wine is pumped direct from the ship. There may be silos into which grain is sucked or enclosed conveyors for taking frozen meat and fresh fruit from ship to shed. The list could be extended to include many other types of storage and cargo handling units.

Right: Grain being sucked out of the hold of a bulk carrier and along a pipe which takes it straight to dockside silos for storage.

Below left: A tanker offloads its cargo of crude oil at a jetty. In some places the jetty may have to be hundreds of yards out to sea.

Below right: A huge floating crane. These are used for loading items such as a locomotive or a heavy piece of machinery.

Above: Icebreakers high and dry for repair in floating docks. Each floating dock is made up of a large ''cradle'' of watertight tanks. This is sunk (by letting water into the tanks) so that the ship can be floated in. Then the water is pumped out and the dock rises, lifting the ship with it. Floating docks can be towed where they are needed. Most large ports also have a dry dock – a concrete basin open to the water at one end only. The ship is sailed in, watertight gates closed, and the water pumped out.

All cargo ships are divided into holds, and the load is arranged to give stability. In the case of general cargo ships, goods for different ports must be loaded in the right order – those for the last port of call first. And care must be taken to avoid contamination (soap must not be stored near food).

Merchant Shipping

Science has changed the merchant seaman's work.
The ship's captain is now in charge of a complex floating machine.

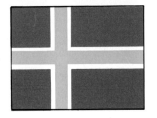

Life at sea was once hard and dangerous. Food was bad, conditions cramped, airless, dark and unhealthy. Punishment was frequent, and death by disease common. Today the merchant seaman's conditions of work and his food are at least as good as those on shore. Modern ships' engines are so efficient that just one engineer officer and one assistant can look after them.

A merchant ship is run on much the same lines as any other business. In command is the captain, or master. Next in line come the navigating or deck officers, and the engineer officers. Navigating officers are responsible for the safe navigation of the ship, and for its maintenance, and the cargo. Navigating officers are often called mates.

Deck hands, or ratings, work for the navigating officers. Their duties include steering, signaling, mooring, handling cargo gear, ropework, and painting. Junior deck hands are called ordinary seamen, and once thex have gained experience and skill they become able seamen. A first class able seaman may be promoted to the job of bosun – short for

The merchant flags of the countries with the largest merchant fleets; in order, top to bottom: Liberia, Japan, Great Britain, Norway

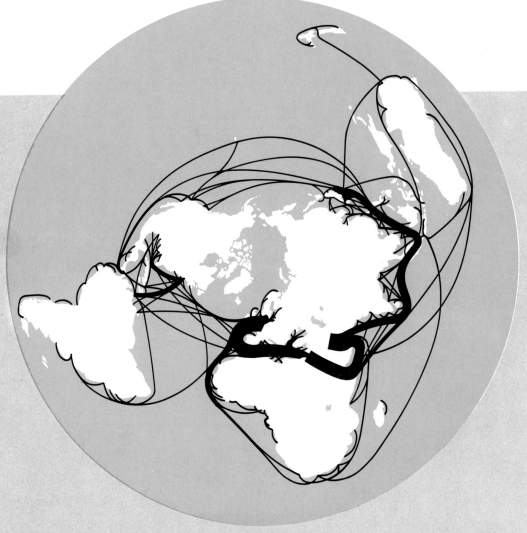

A map of the world's major shipping routes – the thicker the line, the busier the route.

There are nearly 58,000 merchant ships plying the world's oceans. The countries with the largest merchant fleets, and the sizes of those fleets in thousand tons gross, are:

Liberia – 44,444 tons
Japan – 34,929 tons
Great Britain – 28,625 tons
Norway – 23,507 tons
USSR – 16,734 tons
Greece – 15,329 tons
USA – 15,024 tons
West Germany – 8516 tons
Italy – 8187 tons
Panama – 7794 tons
France – 7420 tons
Sweden – 5632 tons
Netherlands – 4972 tons
Spain – 4360 tons
Denmark – 4020 tons

Funnel and flag colors of some of the main passenger ship companies. Left hand column, top to bottom:
1 Cunard Line, Liverpool
2 Shaw Savill Line, Southampton
3 Union-Castle Mail SS Company, London
4 French Line (Compagnie Générale Transatlantique), Le Havre
5 Home Lines Inc., Panama
6 Royal Viking Line, Oslo
7 Peninsular and Oriental Steam Navigation Company, London
8 Hapag-Lloyd AG, Hamburg

Right column, top to bottom:
1 Cie des Messageries Maritimes, Paris
2 British India Steam Navigation Company, London
3 South African Marine Corporation, Cape Town
4 Italia Line, Genoa
5 Holland America Line, Rotterdam
6 Norwegian America Line, Oslo
7 Swedish America Line, Gothenburg
8 USSR (state owned)

boatswain. He is something like a foreman in a factory. The bosun is one of the ship's petty officers. Others include the carpenter, the storekeeper, and the steward.

The engineer officers look after the engines and all the other machinery on the ship. Working for them are the engineer apprentices, firemen and greasers.

The radio officer keeps in touch with shore stations and other ships. He receives weather reports, and keeps a constant watch for distress calls from other vessels. Radio-telephone equipment is used to the full, but Morse Code is still the best way to send messages over long distances. The radio officer must be able to send and receive Morse Code signals at a speed of 20 words a minute.

Flag positions on merchant ships. At the bow the national flag, at the stern, the merchant flag (the two are often the same); on the fore mast, the Mail pennant, and the country of destination; on the bridge, the position for the flags of the International Code of Signals, when used; on the main mast, the shipping line's own flag, and under it the merchant flag is raised when entering or leaving port.

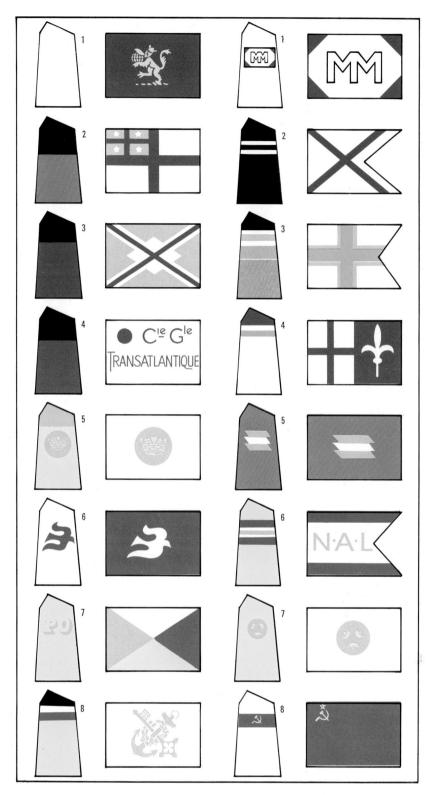

The Story of War at Sea

From the ram bow and the fighting castle to the age of the broadside.

The seamen of the ancient world fought in long ships – sleek, fast, armed with a pointed ram in the bow, and driven by banks of oarsmen. From these ancient biremes and triremes there developed the galleys and galleasses used at the Battle of Lepanto in 1571. This, one of the greatest sea battles of all time, was fought between the combined forces of Spain and Italy, and the 273 galleys of the Turkish fleet led by Ali Pasha.

The galleasses were a cross between galley and galleon. They had the firepower of the galleon and the fast turning power of the galley (which was used for ramming and boarding). They did much to help the allied forces defeat the Turks. But in fact Lepanto was the last great sea battle between rowed ships. The famous Spanish Armada and the British fleet which defeated it in 1588 were made up for the most part of galleons. These galleons were heavily armed sailing ships and, for their day, large ones.

Ships of the Line

Warships from the time of the Armada until the early 19th century remained very much the same. They could only fire broadsides. The big ships sailed into battle in line – hence their name, "ships of the line". A first-rate ship had 100 guns or more, a second-rater between 90 and 100, and a third-rater 50 to 80. Range and accuracy of fire, plus speed were all-important.

Above: An illustration from a book printed in 1585, showing small cannon-balls and much larger "fire bombs" about to hit a ship. Many other kinds of shot were used, including hot shot (solid balls heated until red hot before being put in the gun); and chain shot (two iron balls linked by a chain).

After more than 250 years of the wooden sailing ship and its broadsides, new ideas at last appeared during the mid-19th century. First came the arrival of steam power, and then of the ironclad. The iron armor of these ships gave them a brief advantage. But before long shells were developed which could get through their armor. The real change came at last in 1862, with the launching of the all-iron *Monitor*. She took part in a gunfight with the ironclad *Merrimack* during the American Civil War. Neither ship's guns could penetrate the other's armor. The main point was that *Monitor*'s guns were mounted on a revolving turret.

Now, with steam engines, iron (and soon steel) hulls, and the revolving gun-turret, the stage was set for the great battleships of the early 20th century.

Below: An English man-of-war and Barbary pirates engage in battle. Above: The "Monitor", 1862, the ship which ended the age of the broadside. Her opponent was the "Merrimack".

20th Century Warships

In the struggle for supremacy at sea the submarine has taken over from the battleship.

Above: A modern coastal defense motor torpedo boat which can be quickly converted into a gunboat, a minelayer, or a commando raider. Powered by gas turbine engines, she can exceed 50 knots.

In the past a pitched battle between fleets of heavily armed battleships was the rule of the day in naval warfare. In World War I, on the other hand, Germany and Britain had the most powerful fleets of battleships ever built; yet in the four years of the war they met in a full-scale action only once – at the Battle of Jutland in 1916. After the battle the German fleet returned to harbor and remained there for the rest of the war. The day of the great sea battle between opposed fleets was over. Huge super-battleships were too expensive to risk in a pitched fight, and too easy to attack with submarines and torpedo-carrying cruisers. Instead, they were used in other ways. They were sent out all over the world, a few here, a few there, to seek out and destroy the enemy's big ships. They had to blockade his supplies, and to protect merchant shipping routes. They were also used to guard against invasion, and to protect convoys of ships carrying troops and their supplies. .

By the time of World War II, fighter and bomber aircraft had become the main weapons of war. At sea aircraft carriers and submarines were the navy's main hitting power. Battleships were still needed, to guard convoys against surface raiders and to bombard enemy positions ashore. But many smaller warships were built – corvettes and frigates, specially equipped to hunt submarines. And today it is these smaller ships which form the basis of

Left: HMS ''Dreadnought'', launched in 1906, the first of the great Dreadnought battleships. She carried ten 12-inch guns in five turrets, 24 three-inch guns and five torpedo tubes. She was protected by armor plating nearly one foot thick. Her big guns fired 3000-pound shells and had a range of about eight miles.

most navies. Aircraft carriers are of course the biggest warships of all, but they too are open to attack by missiles and submarines.

Should there be a major war in the future, it would probably be fought above and below the sea. It will be fought by missiles, aircraft and nuclear submarines. Even so, it will always be vital to protect cargo ships carrying supplies. This is the role for which surface warships are now being developed. The largest, the destroyers and cruisers are equipped with few guns but carry many missiles and torpedoes. They can reach speeds of 40 knots or more. Then there are smaller destroyer escorts, anti-aircraft and submarine-killer ships. These are packed with the latest weapons for finding and destroying enemy ships and aircraft. Finally there are the assault ships, carrying perhaps 1000 troops; and landing craft to ferry the troops and their equipment ashore.

Above: A modern anti-aircraft and submarine-killer ship for the defense of merchant convoys. This ship carries an anti-submarine helicopter which can drop homing torpedoes.

Aircraft carriers proved their value in World War II. Their weapons are their aircraft and, today, their guided-missile systems. Catapults and an angled deck enable jet planes to take off and land safely.

Aircraft carriers suffer from one important weakness: they offer the enemy a very large target. None the less, the US Navy built several nuclear carriers, including ''Enterprise'' – the world's longest warship (1101.5 feet).

Submarines and Atoms

Early submarines could stay down for only a short time.
Modern nuclear submarines can cruise underwater for months.

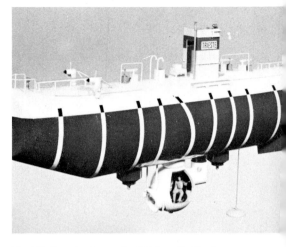

The US Navy bathyscaphe "Trieste". She has reached the deepest part of the ocean bed – 35,802 feet below sea level. The crew ride in the observation cabin under the main hull. The hull is simply a large buoyancy tank filled with gasoline (which is lighter than water). The buoyancy tank also contains ballast tanks.

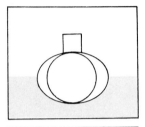

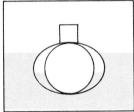

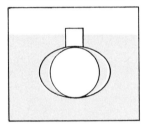

Above: The buoyancy of a submarine is altered by filling the space between the hulls with more or less water.

A submarine is a vessel with two hulls. Its buoyancy can be altered by filling the space between the inner and outer hulls with more or less water. To submerge, water is let into the space; to surface, it is pumped or blown out.

All early submarines were really submersibles – craft which could submerge but which had to surface often to breathe. The first true submarine, able to operate for long periods underwater, was not completed until 1955. The world's first submersible, a one-man midget called *Turtle*, was built in 1775.

Submarines are fitted with pairs of hydroplanes on the sides, forward and aft. These work like an aircraft's ailerons – the hydroplanes can be tilted to make the vessel dive or ascend. Hydroplanes and rudder are linked to a control column similar to that on an aircraft. The helms-

"America's new armored torpedo-boat, the 'Holland'," 1898. The "Holland" submarine had petrol engines for surface running and an electric motor for use when submerged.

Below: A cutaway drawing of a nuclear submarine. The rounded bow and tapering tear-drop shape give maximum speed, stability and control.

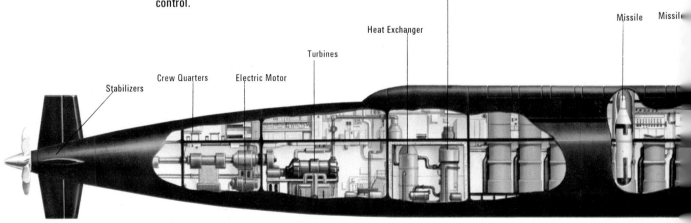

Stabilizers — Crew Quarters — Electric Motor — Turbines — Heat Exchanger — Nuclear Reactor — Missile — Missile

man "flies" his ship through the water by pushing the column forward to dive, pulling it back to climb, and turning its wheel to left or right to turn the ship.

Oil Burning Submarines

Submarines have always been used mainly as warships, since they can easily escape detection by traveling underwater. In the past, submarines had two sets of machinery – diesel engines for cruising on the surface and for charging their batteries, and electric motors for running underwater. Such submarines can cruise underwater for perhaps 48 hours, but after that they must surface to recharge their batteries. During World War II the Germans invented the schnorkel – a pair of tubes sticking up above the surface through which the ship could "breathe in" oxygen and get rid of exhaust gases. So submarines no longer had to surface to recharge, but they had to come up to schnorkel depth – and the schnorkel and its wake could be seen from the air, and detected by surface ships' radar.

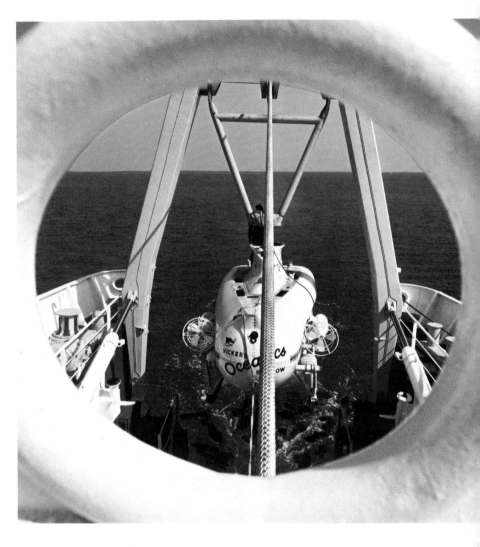

A Pisces submersible being lowered into the sea from its support ship. The submersible can descend to 3000 feet below sea level. It has robot arms, and can go down even in rough weather. It is used for underwater survey, research and rescue work.

The Nuclear Submarine

Nuclear power has solved these problems. A nuclear reactor creates great heat from a tiny amount of fuel, uses no oxygen, and produces no fumes. The enormous difficulties of designing a nuclear reactor small and safe enough for a submarine were overcome by scientists of the US Naval Research Laboratory. The US submarine *Nautilus* – the world's first nuclear-powered ship – was completed in 1955. A nuclear submarine can remain submerged for months on end. In 1960 the US nuclear submarine *Triton* went right round the world underwater, completing 41,500 miles in 83 days.

But a nuclear vessel costs two to four times as much as an ordinary ship. So for merchant ships nuclear power is still too expensive.

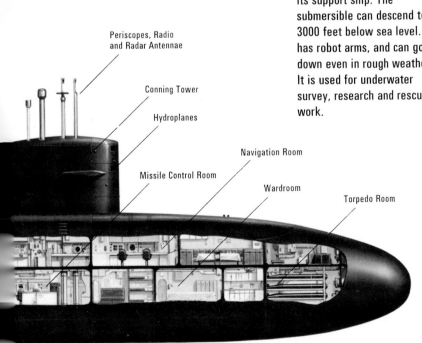

Periscopes, Radio and Radar Antennae

Conning Tower

Hydroplanes

Navigation Room

Missile Control Room

Wardroom

Torpedo Room

The HM2 fixed-sidewall hovercraft. It has rigid sidewalls which project down into the water rather like a pair of keels; flexible skirts are fitted at bow and stern to seal in the "air bubble". Because the sidewalls extend into the water, this type of hovercraft cannot travel over land.

Hydrofoils and Hovercraft

Ships that skim across the surface of the water waste less energy than craft which plow through it.

Shipbuilders generally reckon the top speed of a ship at around 40 to 45 knots. To go faster requires so much more engine power that the cost is too high. Water is over 800 times as dense as air, and the drag on a ship is very much greater than that on a vehicle moving through air. Hydrofoils and hovercraft get over this problem by traveling just above the water.

Hydrofoil craft ride up on underwater wings – the hydrofoils – which project into the water on stalks. At rest a hydrofoil craft sits in the water like any other ship. But as it increases speed the foils provide lift in exactly the same way as an aircraft's wings. The hull rises clear of the water. A hydrofoil ship needs enormous power in relation to its weight, and the stresses on the foils when traveling at speed are very great. So it is unlikely that large, cargo-carrying hydrofoils will be built. But with their speed – 40 to 50 knots is not unusual – and their smooth ride, they make excellent passenger ferry vessels.

At its simplest a hovercraft, or air-cushion vehicle, is a container with no

Below: A diagram of a flexible-skirt hovercraft. The gas turbine engine drives the propellers which move the craft and the fans which lift it. The hovercraft's speed is controlled by altering the pitch (angle) of the propeller blades. To alter course, the pylons on which the propellers are mounted are turned. For a sharp turn the rudder fins are used too.

bottom, fitted with a fan which draws air from above and blasts it downwards. This blast of air lifts the whole thing off the ground. In practice a second 'container' is fitted inside the first, and air is forced down between the two. Much less air has to be moved, and the downward jet coming out all round acts as a curtain. This traps compressed air under the craft and gives greater lift. The SRN1, the first hovercraft to cross the English Channel (in 1959), worked on this principle. But the lift was not enough for anything but a fairly calm sea. This problem was solved by fitting flexible rubber "skirts" (see diagram). The skirts bend out of the water when the hovercraft

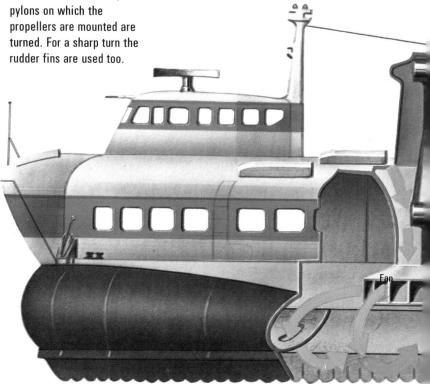

Fan

meets a wave, or any other obstacle. The flexible-skirt hovercraft is equally at home traveling over land or sea. This is the type of hovercraft in general use today as a passenger vehicle and as a fighting "ship". It can travel at speeds of 60 or even 100 knots.

At slow speeds hovercraft make a bow wave and a wake, just like a ship. But once the craft reaches a certain speed it climbs on top of its bow wave. From that point on it has only to contend with air friction. There is no wake, "just water stroked by a shaving brush" as Christopher Cockerell, the hovercraft's inventor, said on the first cross-channel trip.

Left: Most early hydrofoils had ladder-like foils (top). The two types used today are the "surface-piercing" (middle) and the "fully submerged" (lower).

Top: A flexible-skirt hovercraft ferry. Above: The Soviet surface-piercing hydrofoil ferry on Lake Baikal in the USSR. Craft like this can cruise at around 35 knots, and are ideal on calm inland waters or sheltered seas.

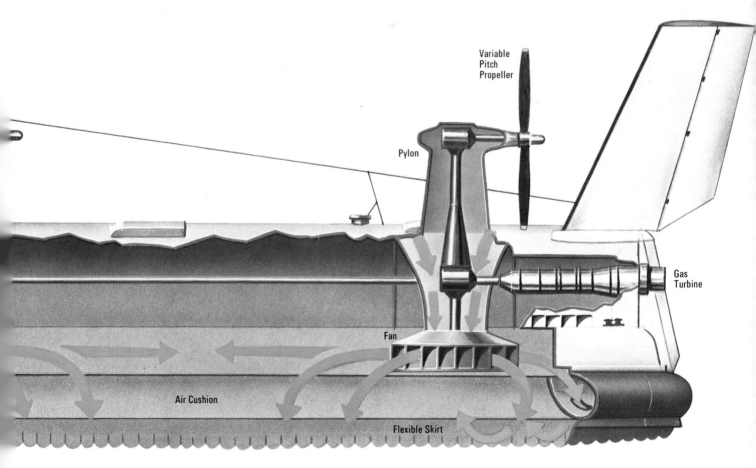

Variable Pitch Propeller

Pylon

Gas Turbine

Fan

Air Cushion

Flexible Skirt

Glossary of Terms

Brig

Brigantine

Lugger

Lateen

Cutter

A

Abaft Behind, towards the stern.
Abeam Across the ship, at right angles to its length.
Aft At or near the stern of a ship.
Ahead Directly in front of the bows.
Amidships In the middle of a ship.
Anchor Heavy piece of iron which digs into the sea bed to hold a ship to the spot.
Astern Backwards – behind the stern.
Athwartships Across the ship, from one side to the other.
Awash Level with the surface of the sea.

B

Ballast Heavy material (often water) carried in ship's hold to give stability.
Beam Width of ship at its widest point.
Berth Place where a ship ties up.
Bilge The bottom of a ship.
Boom A pole along the foot of a sail.
Bow The front of a ship.
Bowsprit Long pole projecting from the bow, on which sails are fixed.
Bow thrusters Small propellers in the bows to help steering at low speeds.
Bridge Raised deck from which a ship is navigated.
Bulkhead Wall dividing up the inside of a ship.
Bulwark Low "wall" of steel plating along side of deck, for safety of passengers and crew.
Buoy A floating marker moored in the water to guide or warn ships.
Buoyancy The ability of an object to float.

C

Capstan A small winch.
Carvel-built (Of a wooden ship): having its planks laid edge to edge.
Cavitation The formation of hollows (cavities) of air around a ship's propeller when it turns very fast.
Chart Map of the sea and coastal waters.
Clinker-built (Of a wooden ship): having its planks overlapping.
CODOG Combined diesel and gas turbine propulsion.
COGOG Gas turbine propulsion.
Companion Stairway leading below from the deck, with weatherproof entrance.

Conning tower The superstructure of a submarine.
COSAG Combined steam and gas turbine propulsion.
Crosstrees Small platform at masthead.

D

Deck Floor.
Derrick A kind of crane mounted on many cargo ships.
Dock The working area of a harbor where ships are loaded and unloaded.
Draft Depth of a ship below the water.
D.w. or **d.w.t.** Deadweight tonnage.

F

Fathom Unit of length used for measuring the depth of water, equal to six feet.
Fore Nearest to the bows.
Forecastle, or **Fo'c'sle** Raised deck in the bows. Often used to describe accommodation in the bows.
FPB Fast patrol boat.
Freeboard Height from waterline to the top of the hull
Funnel A ship's chimney or smokestack.

G

Galley A ship's kitchen.
Galleon Large sailing ship with high bow and stern.
Gear Nautical word for machinery or equipment – e.g. steering gear, ship's gear (derricks, cranes etc. for loading cargo).
G.r.t. Gross registered tonnage.
Gunwale Upper edge of the side of a ship.

H

Hatch Opening or door in deck or side.
Helm Steering control of a ship.
Hogging The tendency of a ship to droop at bow and stern when it rides over a wave.
Hold Space below deck for cargo.
Hull The body of a ship.
Hydroplane Underwater "wing" on a submarine, for controlling angle of "flight".

I

Ironclad Warship with covering of iron plates for protection from gunshot.
Island Raised part of a ship's hull.

K

Keel The main piece of steel (or wood) along a ship's bottom, from stem to stern.
Knot A measure of speed – one nautical mile an hour.

L

LASH Lighter Aboard Ship vessel
Lateen A type of triangular fore-and-aft sail.
Latitude Distance north or south of the equator, measured in degrees, from 0° on the equator to 90° at the poles.
Leeward Direction towards which the wind blows. The lee side of a ship is therefore the sheltered side, away from the wind.
Load lines Lines painted on the side of ships to show how deeply they may safely be loaded.
Longitude Distance east or west of the Greenwich zero meridian, measured in degrees east or west of Greenwich.

M

Mizzen Fore-and-aft sail on aftermost mast.
Moor To secure a ship, either against a quay, or by tying it to a mooring buoy, or by dropping anchor.
MTB Motor Torpedo Boat.
MV Motor vessel – i.e. a ship with diesel, not steam, engines.

N

Nautical mile A measure of distance, equal to 1/60 of a degree of latitude, or 6080 feet.
N.r.t. Net registered tonnage.

O

OBO Oil/Bulk/Ore ship – a type of bulk cargo ship equipped to carry various bulk cargoes.

P

Pilot Seaman licensed to navigate ships into and out of port. Once out to sea, the captain takes over and the pilot returns to shore.
Pilothouse Enclosed space on upper deck from which the ship is steered.
Pitching The plunging and rising movements of a ship as it rides across the waves.
Poop A raised deck at the stern.

Port The left-hand side of a ship, looking forward.
Porthole An opening in the side of a ship to let in light and air.
PS Paddle steamer.

Q

Quarterdeck Upper deck running from stern to mainmast. Also, a part of the deck reserved for officers.

R

Rake The slope of masts, funnels, bows, etc.
Rigging Wires and ropes used to control sails, masts and other spars.
Rudder Flat blade of wood or metal at the stern which is turned to steer a ship.

S

Screw Underwater propeller used to move a ship.
Scuppers Openings in the ship's sides or bulwarks to allow water to run off the deck (also called freeing or wash ports).
Sextant An instrument used mainly to measure the height of the sun and stars above the horizon.
Side thruster Another name for bow thruster.
Spar Metal or wooden pole used as mast, yard, gaff, boom etc.
SS Steam ship.
Starboard The right-hand side of a ship, looking forward.
Stay Fore-and-aft rope supporting a mast or spar.
Stem Curved post at the bow to which side plates or planks are fixed.
Stern The back of a ship.
Superstructure The parts of a ship built on above the main deck (as distinct from islands, which are an integral part of the hull).

T

Tiller Length of wood on the top of the rudder, for turning it.
Topside The part of a ship's sides above the waterline.
Tramp A cargo ship which, instead of following a regular route, plies for trade wherever there is work.
Trim The way a ship floats in the water (on an even keel, down at the bow or stern, etc.).

W

Wake or **Wash** The waves and foam caused by a moving ship.
Watch A spell of duty for a seaman.
Well deck A deck between two islands.
Windward Direction from which the wind blows. The windward side is therefore the one exposed to the wind.

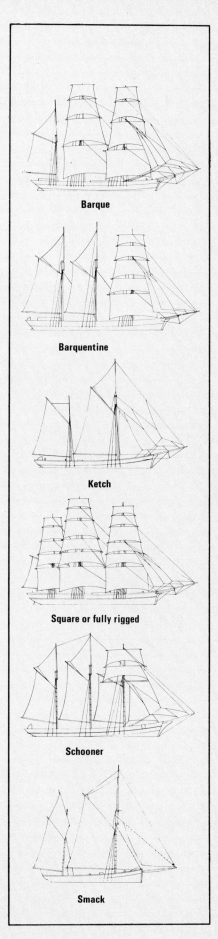

Barque

Barquentine

Ketch

Square or fully rigged

Schooner

Smack

Index

Acknowledgments

Photographs: Page 2 British Hovercraft Corporation (top), Vickers (bottom & center); 3 P & O Lines (bottom); 4 P & O Lines (top & center), Yarrow (Shipbuilders) Ltd (bottom); 6 Vickers; 8 P & O Lines (top right), Vickers (top left & right); 9 Vosper Thornycroft Ltd; 10 Science Museum (top & center); 12 Sperry Marine Systems (top); 13 Sperry Marine Systems (bottom & center); 15 Maritime Safety Agency, Tokyo (bottom), Sperry Marine Systems (top), US Coast Guard (center); 16 Aerofilms (left), Tate Gallery (bottom); 17 The Salvage Association (top & bottom); 18 J. Allan Cash; 19 Michael Holford; 20 Mansell Collection (top), Michael Holford (bottom); 21 Michael Holford (bottom); 22 Mary Evans Picture Library (bottom), National Maritime Museum (top), 23 National Maritime Museum; 25 National Maritime Museum; 26 Mansell Collection; 27 Mary Evans Picture Library; 28 Barnaby's Picture Library (bottom), P. Morris (top), Radio Times Hulton Picture Library (center); 29 Radio Times Hulton Picture Library; 30 Mosvold Shipping Co. Norway; 31 Globtik Tankers London Ltd. (top), J. Allan Cash (left), Swan Hunter Group Ltd. (center), Vickers (bottom), 32 Scripps Institute, California; 33 Cable & Wireless (top), Danish State Railways (bottom), Novosti (right); 34 Port of London Authority (top), Vickers (bottom); 35 Port of London Authority (bottom right), Shell (bottom left), Spillers Limited (center), Vickers (top); 39 National Maritime Museum (bottom); 41 Science Museum (top); 42 Mary Evans Picture Library; 43 Vickers; 44 Hovermarine Transport Ltd. (top); 45 Novosti.

Picture Research: Penny Warn & Jackie Newton.